# HAIL SA

## A COLLECTION OF SA
## MYKHAILO CH
### ILLUSTRAT
### M.B.

for Masha

I.H. Publishing

Hail Satan
©2009 Mykhailo Chornyisyn
All rights reserved
Illustration by M.B.
ISBN 978-0-557-06489-2
First Edition 2009

# EVOCATION

LUCIFER ✳ OUIA ✳ KAMERON
ALISCOR ✳ MANDUSEMINI ✳ POEMI
ORIEL ✳ MADUGRUSE ✳ PARINOSCON
ESTIO ✳ DUMOGON ✳ DOVORCON
CASMIEL ✳ HUGRAS ✳ FABIL ✳ VONTON
ULI ✳ SOCIERNO ✳ PÈATAN!
COME LUCIFER.

ABSOLUTE HATRED
LANCEA
SKELOKOPEIN CONSOLATION
SIGH MIGHTY KABBĀBĀ
CASTE AND STAGE ATOM CAST
WHY OFFER HIM A PEARL?

tetragrammaton NAY
NONE POSSESS OUR HOME
NOR COMB TO IMPAIR
COMMON CRIMINAL
DISGRACEFUL DILETTANTE
SHAME FOR SHAME
YOUR CONDUCT

ɔb COLLAPSE WORN
MAGICK SEWN BLACK
COME SEE BARK THE WORD
LIVE BELLOW BE DONE
QUASH ONUS
TENDER LIFE TO NONE

ONE WANDERED PRESAGE OF LORE
GHOST ALLEGED HOLY DEFLORATING NORNS
AVERSE ENCOUNTER POWER
ABUSE WILL REST THE SCORE
BOILING PUISSANCE UNYIELDING
THE VENGEFUL CELESTIAL HORDE
NE'ER LAPSING AUGHT NOWISE BEGAN

SERAPH SPURNING THE CONCEPT OF SIN
INGESTED KEYS PASS TAPERED GRIN
TWO STAND BACKWARD BEAUTIFUL TWINS
THE HEIRS OF ATARAXIA'S END

*MALEFICUS* MY FONDNESS
I HAVE SPADE THE SEA FROM A POND
SPITTING SULLIED SEED
LIMITLESS SWELL
SING LEGACY'S SONG
"CRIPPLE THE RIGHTEOUS" ABSCOND
GOOD GONE FRAIL FAMILY
WE HAVE OUR OWN
SHADOW SHOW
THE MARROW OF OS

MY FATHER EVIL
TUTELAR OF SELF
MY BROTHER HATRED
WHOSE WINGS ARE TWELVE
YOUR FREEDOM IS PROVINCE
AS MY NEEDS ARE MET
LIFE MINUS CHANCE
IN AIR WITHOUT WAGER

TOMORROW IS CERTAIN
YOUR LATITUDE IS HERE
MY DURESS WILL CONFOUND
YOUR TURNKEY, THE WARDEN
AND HIS PEERS
THEIR BROOD CRUCIFIES ANYONE
TO MAKE THEIR POINT CLEAR
MY WILL DOES NOT WAVER
THEY SHALL EMBRACE FEAR

FUCK YOU SUNSHINE
YOU SMELL LIKE DICK
SPANGLED PLACENTA

LIFE AT LENGTH IS ABRUPT
LIGHT FICTIVE
LUCENT KNOWLEDGE A WALL
LET THERE BE SILENCE
AS IT WAS BEFORE
CONCERTED TINKLE
HUSH I HEAR MUTE MEMOIRE

STARE

PISSING SUNSHINE MOUNT THINE FIST
CHAOS ROOK THE SEELED
BÊTE NOIRE TROUVÉS ARMOUR
TIGHT FIT, THROWN
QUIESCE AND RESEED
MEMO:  FOR THE FUTURE
DEBTS NEED BE PAID
ILLUMINATE FICTIONAL RAGE
SOME DO NOT SEE SO LIGHT
THE DEBTORS TREASURY DRY

SON IS SHINING

I REMEMBER YOUR SUIT
I REMEMBER YOUR PRIDE

A SHAME HAS RIPENED
IN OUR PRECIOUS ZONE
NEGLIGENCE IS STUNTING GROWTH
I WILL TRAIPSE UPON BONES
CONSCIOUS OF THE BASAL PLANE
PATRONIZING GHOSTS
AND DEMONS IF YOU PLEASE
THEIR WRATH COMFORTS ME
HOWEVER THAT MAY BE
MY IMPETUS PALISADE
ATOP WE REMAIN
NO, I AM NOT PETITIONED
NO, I DO NOT PERCEIVE

GRIEF HAS GROWN FATIGUED
DISMAY A NEW BELIEF
PATIENCE IS VERIFIED
IN TERRENE SCHEME
HERE IS WHAT I LEAVE
MORALS - MORTALS
TURNED INSIDE OUT
AS THIS IS WRITTEN
A CHILD NEAR ME POUTS
THE GAMIN LUCIFER
MAGICKAL DEVOID OF TEARS
FALLING WIND
JOY IS HERE
WAFTING THROUGH INIQUITY

THE BITCH SAID
MAN TAKE THIS PLANET
CHOKING ON HIS GUILT
TOO TERRIFIED TO REVEAL
AN OPERATION HAD PASSED
WHISPERING CREATION
DOOMED TO MURMUR
MURDEROUS JOKES
THE BITCH SAID
MAN DON'T LET ME CHOKE
WHAT MAN
HEED MY EQUIVALENCE
I AM OVER
LOUD THE BITCH BOASTS
LO! WEASEL EXPLODES
I COME HEARING EVIL
FUCK ALL THESE PEOPLE
KING BITCH HUNG
FROM THE STEEPLE
POPINGO... BOWMAN
ARROW NARROW
KEYHOLE PEER

BOLD UNCLE BOTCH
SURRENDER THE GLITCH
AMASS AND BARRACADE
FEARING RUIN BRACE
NOTHING IS NEARING
NOTHING WITH JAWS
EVERYONE HAS HUNGERED
THE HUMANS ALL ALONG
ONE LINE LEADS TO THE VIRGIN ARC
YOUR LINES DRIFT IN OUR WATER
POLLUTING ALL WE DRINK
INFECTING REASON
YOUR LINES SINK
INTERVENE WIDOWERED
LEVIATHAN
CHAOTIC TIAMAT
PASSAGES PROMPTLY EBBING
TRANSCENDENT SEAL SO LEAN
OVER AND OVER A WELL
OUR QUILL
WE ARE WRITING YOU THIS LETTER
FROM HELL

# THE GLOBAL VILLAGE

CALLING ALL EARTH
CALLING ALL EARTH

SURFACE MALFUNCTION
RACE OF HUMANS

EXTINGUISH

THEY ARE KNOWN TO BE WEAK
THEIR RELIGIONS AND WEAPONS
ARE NOT CHILD PROOF

SURFACE MALFUNCTION
A.P.B.
*ALL PEOPLE BURN*

TO SUMMON SÆMʃAʔel
AND FAMOUS WAKE
YOU MAY CALCULATE FATE SEDATELY
BANE HOVERING
DIM BEACON
SOBER INTOXICATING QUESTIONS
SPEAKING OUT LOUD OF DEATH
KINDLE THE FIRES LO' SET
ONE HOME MAY BE DESTROYED
SO WILL THE REST
FUEL FOR SUN
CENTER OF DESTRUCTION
SPIRITLESS CORPSE
HUMAN FOLLOW THE MOON
COMFORT YOUR BRUISE
DAINTY DELICATE MUSE
CONQUEST OF PLANETS
FORM IMMEDIATE CONSUMED
AND HUMAN
DO NOT SEEK TO RETURN
SUMMATION THICKEN
THOSE WHO STAY
WHEN DESTINY IS DISARRAY
CONQUER MEW
WHILE SEEKING CIRCLES
NOT FOUND IN CORNERS

VOMIT GOES AROUND
PUKE LIKE A BICYCLE WHEEL
LIVES ARE REACTIONS
KINESIS, PEDESTRIAN AND MUNDANE

WE REQUIRE GIFTS FOR DEEDS
WORDS MEAN NOTHING
WORDS ARE RELIEF
WE COMMUNICATE THE SAME

I DEMAND SELF
WHILE DEFENDING ALL ELSE
LIKE EVERYONE SO SELFISH
QUANTUM AND PARALLEL

I KNOW I AM NOT DIFFERENT
I KNOW THERE IS NO CHANCE
I HARNESS ONE POWER
IN DIRE CIRCUMSTANCE

GO TO THE OLD TOMORROW
WHERE YOU SEE YOURSELF
SCULPT SILENCE
BE ALONE

DO ANYTHING FOR NO-ONE
UNTO NOTHING OR NOWHERE
ACKNOWLEDGE HALLUCINATION
NEVER SPEAK OF YOUR OWN

I DO NOT HAVE A PRAYER
GLAD
I DO NOT WANT ANYTHING
LEAVE

I WILL ROT AND CEASE
YOU MAY HAVE EVERYTHING
I DO NOT SEEK

SURROUNDED BY UNFAMILIARITY
NAUGHT NOW NEW
HEART INVERT HANG
MIGHT FALL FURTHER
STILL WELL NOTHING MOVE
ELEMENTAL HELL
COMFORTABLE BAD
IN UNIVERSAL PIT

I DESERVE:
LIFE THE TRAP TO LIVE WITHOUT
A FROZEN MIRROR
AN ETERNAL MAP

HEALTHY REACTION
HATE
ISOLATE THE DIAPHANOUS
HATE BE BRAVE

RAVAGE AT WILL SHAMELESS
CONFIDE IN INFINITE ENMITY
NEVER COMMUNICATE
INDIGNATION'S EXPRESSION

AFTERDEATH
HATE-AFTER LIFE
LOATHE AS YOU LIKEN
ASSIMILATE WITH ANIMALS
TAME HUMANS
DEMAND REPRISAL
COUNSEL SAMAEL'S RACE
TO ACCEPT HATRED
NEVER TO ESCAPE

# ALL IS DONE

NOW COME -
IN LIVING MAN MADE PROMISE
TO COMFORT A DAY STAR
TOURNICATE THE BLEEDING
BROKEN BROW COME NOW - SPEAK
YOU CHOOSE AUTONOMY,
"FREE 'MY BROTHER LUCIFER."
HERE WHAT I DO
UPHOLD AXIOM
CIRCUMVENT BAIT
DEAF WHEN BECKONED
STREAM WINDING LAMENT
LIGHT AND MIGHT
LESS OUR FEW
DIFFUSE UPSTREAM
LEFT COLTER IN HAND
FISSURES ANEW
RETRIBUTE?
NOTARIZE NO REGRESSION
OUR MOMENT TO ALIGN
DEATH WE MUST SHARE
NE'ER BREAK BREAD WITH SHEEP
ALL OF WHOM SHALL BE SHEARED

SWEAT SO RUN FAST
AWAY, AWAY SHEPHERD
DISCOVER SWEET CHAOS
THE CLIFFS REJOICE THY NAME
BEINGS BEING GATHERED

BENIGN DOUBTFUL ILLUSIONIST
HEADLESS MAGUS
ENTICE THE FIT FOOL UNTO
MARVELOUS APPARATUS
NAIL THEM TO YOU
THRONE THROWN
SET FIRE TO THE PEWS

CALLOUS COMPREHENSION
MALIGN IN NATURE
TIME HAS BENT
THE SUN OF THE WEST

CUNNING CLAY SACROSANCT TALES
Ô COURT FALL TO FAIL?
EVERYONE IS FOR SALE
MY TAG WENT UNMARKED
BESTIAL INTEREST MATURE
SIGHT SUPERSEDE ETERNITY
THERE IS JUSTICE IN THE DARK

# LA VIDA

BREATHE OUR FUME
IN FLIGHT PURE PLUME
THE STOCKADE - THE NURSERY
MERCENARY LIQUIDATE christ
RANSOM ABANDONED
TIME REIMBURSE LIFE
COCKED HAND
STRIKE THE PIOUS
FEED ON FIRE

TURN FROM THE CENTER
FEAR'S DESIROUS MIDWAY
FOLLOW PARALLEL
UNTIL WE DEPART
TO RESOLVE THE DAWN

THE CLERIC TAKES IT EASY
THE DEVICE OF MOTHERS AND QUEENS
THE RELIC SWADDLED IS REMINDER
THE TIARA INFAMY
FOR THE PERJURER KING
OF IMPALED KINGS

DO WE FEEL SOMETHING,
WHAT TELLS US TO RESPOND?
ENJOY SOMETHING WRONG
FROM YOUR PAST
MOLESTING REGRET
I CAN FEEL A LOVING TOUCH
REACHING FOR ME STRANGE
OAFISH DESIRE OR MORE
DARKENING WEALTH ON EARTH
AND REACHING, THE ACT
I AM MORE

WHEN I ENDEAVOR SO MUCH
WHEN I SENSE TOO MUCH
AND I HAVE SAID ENOUGH
REACHING TEETERING
UPROOTING VIRTUE
I CANNOT DIE
WITHOUT THE WISDOM OF EMBRACE
FOR ONE SEAL UPON MY HEART

COME DOWN
DEAR WINDING ROAD
CALM DOWN

DEWY VERDURE
TOO HEAVY FOR THE TREE
TURN GROUND
TO PLOW HOMES
OF HOUSE SOUND
SHELTERED MIND

DEW CAVES KNOW
DISTANCE FINE
TERMINAL RACE
FINALITY LAITY FORSAKE
CALLING UNTO

HOW PERFECT THEY MATE
GAZING AT ONE ANOTHER
MOST OF THEM
SACRIFICE THEIR MOTHERS
SOME KNOW WIND
WANT TO PREVENT BROTHERS
FROM SHUTTING THE DOOR
TO A ROOM WHERE THEY SUFFER

PAT ON THE BACK KID
YOU DID GOOD
WHAT ANY RIGHT CITIZEN WOULD
WITH A GUN IN THEIR GOB
MY WHAT A THICK BARREL YOU HAVE
WHAT'S A CITIZEN LIKE YOU
DOING IN A SUICIDE LIKE THIS?
SHOULDN'T YOU GO
PRACTICE HANGING
SHOULDN'T YOU BE
DEAD BY NOW?

O' YOU DID GOOD KID
CITIZENS ARE RIGHT
HERE IN MURDERWORLD
WE GET TO KILL EACH OTHER

WARRING WANTON WHITE
TO THE EARTH
IN SPITE OF HUMANITY
WE WILL STAY
THIS WORLD
DEVOID OF PIGMENT
CONCEALING TRACKS
SHADOWS AND SHAPES

VISUALIZE
THE STATE YOU ARE IN
ANYTHING YOU INFUSE
WILL BE LORN
BY THOSE SIMPLY SEIZED
IN ARGENTIA

BEDIM HINTERLAND
ALL REMAIN AWAKE
TRUST
TO KILL
RESPLENDENT
IN BROAD DAY LIGHT

CHILD OF THE NIGHT
YOU MUST RISE UP AND FIGHT
FOR YOU ARE EVIL
EYE FOR AN EYE
IN THE LIGHT
SATAN'S PEOPLE
...WOE

THE HILLS ARE ALIVE
WITH THE SMELL OF BLOOD
FROM WEAPONS SHARPENED
IN BATTLE
FOE
THIS IS WHY WE HAVE COME
TO LAY WASTE OF THIS LAND
AND ALL THESE CREATURES

...SOW

PESTILENCE AND GERM UPRISE
VINE-RIPENED IN ANOXIC WATERS
TO MARKET, TO DEFECATE
ON THE DEEDS OF EARTH'S LEADERS

GO.
FROM THE CLIFF
TERMINATE ANGELIC LIES
AND DISMANTLE THEIR SAVIOUR

YOUR HONOR I STAND, BE FORTRESS
THIS RIDICULOUS SAFE HARBOR
A MASSIVE MANNEQUIN
STUFFED WITH MORALITY
COMPARTMENTALIZED
OPERATIVE HUMAN RESPONSE CATALOG

THE APPARENT MOTIVATION
TO RULE APLOMB
TO JUSTIFY VIOLENCE
IN EXPONENTIAL TRIALS
COURTING WARFARE
ARBITRARY MAGNITUDES

GRAND NATURAL DISASTER
INVENTED - PAID FOR
FOSTERED BY HUMANKIND
OUTSIDE OF COMMUNITY
FORT B

ÆON
THE SAME RULERS
THE SERFS IDENTICAL
NO MORE QUESTIONS
YOU HAVE DONE WELL
QUELLING ANSWERS
SHALL I SIT STILL?
LEAVE ME UPRIGHT
WITNESS IRE ETERNAL

THE PREY WILL PRAY
WHAT ART IS
DEATH MIGHT FORGIVE
WHO IS THERE PISSING GUILT
SOME GRAND WIZARD
TWADDLING BEHIND A FIG
LEAFING THROUGH DOGMA
THROWING POTTERY
TO EXTERMINATION
COMPOUNDED SENTIENCE
SOVEREIGN DAMAGE

FACULTY OF DOCTRINE'S DOOM

NOTHING GAINED
MY MENTATION
FAR FROM MISFIRING
REANIMATE CORE
MINDFUL AIM
ENTER BETWIXT
FOLDED HANDS
REACH AND STAND
FACING A GRAND WIZARD
IN HIS ESTATE

THE HOME THRONE WILL BE SMELT
TO FASHION A RAVISHING CUP
MY BROTHER AND I DRINK FROM

POL SERVICE ME
IN DIRE CIVIC DUTY
AND INQUIRE
HOW OR WHO FOR?
"THE INTRODUCTION OF LUCIFER"
R.S.V.P. EVISCERATING GALA

WITH PAMPHLETS ERECT
SEEKING PROVIDENCE
COLLECTIVE DENIAL ROOTS
ALL THAT IS NOBLE
ecclesiastical

WILL DISMISS CHALLENGE
DETERMINATE SET LIFE
TO IMPART INCLINATION
TO CONFRONT DOMINATION
WITH INCESSANT PRIDE

NO LOITERING LIGHT LOVER
HOVER UNTO OTHER SIDES
WHERE BACKWARD LIFE
FINDS YOU BEATIFIC AND RIGHT

LATITUDE SLEEVE
ONE MAN'S FREEDOM
IS ANOTHER'S BEAST
SO WHY NOT MOCK LIBERATION
AND POISON DOVES?
PULL... LET THEM FLY
INTO A FIRE FIGHT

WE ROUTE OUR LIVES SEPARATELY
WHILE FLEETING DESIRE
PRODS US TO UNITE
THE HOPE FOR A WORLD
FILLED WITH LIGHT
BRIMMING OBLIGATORY
PLAIN PROSAIC SIGHTS
THIS IS NOT RIGHT

ALL OBJECTS CHARGED
SHROUDED IN SUBCONSCIOUS VAUNT
CAREENING THROUGH MEGACOSMS
Ô EYES MEMORIZE
THE WORST OF WITCH
HAG HUNT FOR SWAG
COME FOR ME DECAYED
SEVEN BILLION DEAD
I AM NOT RIGHT

# MARTY

LOOK AT MARTIN STAPLED TO THE WALL
HOW CURIOUS IN NATURE
BUTTERFLY FALL
FOR SCIENCE AND COLOSSAL MICROSCOPE
I WOULD HAVE TIED HIM UP
SHOT HIM FULL OF DOPE

WHAT OF MARTY'S JAILING?
WHERE IS HIS PUPIL PETER?

SAGA MOTHERFUCKER
WINGED INSECTA
NO PRISONS HOLD
THEY ARE BEAUTIFUL
HAMMERED TO WALLS
FOR TWO THOUSAND YEARS
SOMEONE HAS BALLS
RIB AND STALK
OUTLINE THE CROSS IN CHALK
SUCCESS IS NOT FREEDOM
DEBT IS SUPERNATURAL
EVERLASTING EARTHLY PROTECTORATE
SUMMON ANGELIC HAVOC

# JOHN HAS DROWNED

SAINTLY, QUAINT THE DOILY
JOHN THE DOLLY
PATRON OF A MASS BROTHY GRAVE
HE LOST HIS HEAD IN A DISH
AEROBIC EMBRYO
HE HAS BEEN DROWNED
IN SIGHT OF HIS FATHER
MASSAGING HIS BROTHER
THE STUDENT FELLATING HIS TEACHER
A PASTRY FLAKEY
DUNKING THE PUPIL
SWALLOWING PRIDE
AND WATER
christ COCK SHOWERS
DAMPENED CONTRARY
SEALING THE NEOPHYTE'S DEMISE
JOHN STAY DOWN
THE SERVICE PLATTER IS TAWDRY
STICKS OUT LIKE HOMOSEXUAL CLERGY
LOVE IS VIOLENCE
EUƏ *OXYS GENĒS*
REPLENISH YOUR LUNGS
WITH SWEET AQUA PURA

MOLTEN, WINNOW MY CHORD AGAIN
PROGENY BUOYANT WITH PRIDE
EARTH IS ALRIGHT
HOW TO FLY
HUNT SOME FOR THE TRIBE
GLORIFY HARASSMENT, VANDALIZE
IN THE WORST WAY I LANGUISH
FOR DESTRUCTION
               FAMILY CONVERGE
                   EN MASSE

    QUESTION[2]
    WHAT WINGS ARE LEFT
    MY SWORD AND SHIELD?
I FORFEIT SCYTHE
FOR MY BROTHER
MY PAVISE HIS PRIDE
ONCE I DID NOT SOAR
MY DOMAIN RIMA
SEQUEL OF LIGHT
THE MORNING SORTIE
Ô STARS KNOW
WINDS OF WINGED MIGHT
ECLIPSE HEAVEN WITHOUT MENTION
SPY TO THE SKIES
PERMIT STRENGTH A CRISP COMA
WHILE WINGS RAPE TIME
TO VOYAGE A VILE ASCENT

O' DANNY BOY EDEN
EDEN IS CALLING
the lion of the tribe of judah
PETITIONS AUDIENCE
BEELZEBUB ATTEND
COLD AMBITION
RENOVATE TEMPTATION
AVOWING HAUTEUR
THE LION'S PRIDE
WE REQUIRE TAPESTRY
TO ADORN THE LOESS

WE NURTURE OUR ANCESTORS
UNDER THE FLOOR
A DAM IN NOD
A DROUGHT IN PARADISE
A FLAYING OF THE PRIDE
AMOUR-PROPRE CEDE
MANE RISE NEVERMORE
DECORATE THE LANDSCAPE
TROPHY WHORE

BEAR IN MIND
WE EXHALT LUCIFER
FEASTING ON the lion of judah

# ENDEMIC DIURNAL COURSE

NO HUMAN IS CLOSE
AS FIERY JACKYLS CONVENE
BEAST SET BLACK
TAKE YOUR TIME
QUIETLY CELEBRATE
YOUR SELF AND THE MASSACRED
                           ALLEGIANCE

THEY BORE TUNNELS
IN HUMAN MINDS UNDER LAND
FAR FROM SEA'S EMBRACE
HUMANS COZEN WITH HAND
AND WORSE THEY FEED
I AM WORSHIPPING ME
I HAVE EVERYTHING
I DO NOT NEED
AND I AM NOT HAPPY
AND I AM NOT WHERE YOU ARE
AND I WANT TO KILL EVERYONE

MARCH AND CLAMP
THE NECK AND GRIP
AIR LOSS
NOWHERE LEFT TO LEVITATE
THE TRAIL HAVING PAST
COMPLICATE.
MASTERS AWAKE
THESE WILL BE OUR NIGHTS
WITH THE PERFECTION
OF DISOBEDIENCE
WE MARK OUR TERRITORY
AND GRIP THE NECK
MANIFEST AMBUSH
IN PRIDEFUL VESTMENTS
- FORMAL ATTIRE -
HONOR NOX & STRIKE
FOR ACCOUNT ETERNAL
ALL OF US TOGETHER
WILL KILL EVERYTHING

THE GRIND IS DONE HERE
ELSEWHERE I WANDER
TO DAWN I KNOW WELL
THIS IS MY FAVORITE PART
THE YEARS ARE PLANNED
AND DAYS TO THE NEXT DAY
PICTURESQUE ALL PARTS
PART AWAY DRAWN APART
PAINTED PAINTS PARTING
BRUSH AGAINST ME NO MORE
AND STRETCH NO FURTHER
MY GRIND IS DONE
HEAD OF MY INNATE LEAGUE
TOLERATE
TAKE MY INSIDES
PRESERVE THEM
CHERISH MY RESISTANCE
STOIC NOURISHMENT BEQUEATHED
DRIVE THE ANLACE THROUGH ME
DROP THE HATCH OF MY CASKET
THERE IS NO NAME FOR ME
FEAR IS EAVESDROPPING
MY VACANT AWE
GALENA WHET TODAY
DENSE DISPLAY A BLAZEN TAX
HALE LURID WISDOM
END ALL

HUMANOID MAIM SILENCE
BEFORE THEM PROMISE
WRITTEN IN WASTE
THEY SERVE AS SLAVES
UNTO BORDERLANDS
VESSELS AWASH WITH
CURSE AFTER CURSE
ABOMINATIONS BETROTH
CONJURED FROM DIRE SOURCE
WEAKENED BY TRUTH
ENNOBLE NOTHINGNESS FROM BEING
WELKIN IDOLATOR
I COME FROM NOWHERE
WITNESS NOTHING
HOLDING WHAT I HAVE
SERVANT METATRON'S CHAPERONE
NIHIL A MEN
THE SWAIN LIFELESS BEFORE ME
EYE MORE THAN I; SCRIBE
INHERIT THE HEINOUS HOARD
BUCKLER AND BLADE PARADIGM
FOR FREEDOM
FOR LUCIFER
AND FOR ALL OF TIME

AT THE SHORES WE HAD
NOWHERE TO GO
IN THE MOUNTAINS WE BURIED
OUR LOVE
TO THE FOREST WE RAN
BALING ORDNANCE
AT DAWN WE LOADED
WAKEFUL WEAPONS
ONE BY ONE
WE SHOT EACH OTHER
ABUNDANT AMMUNITION
ECLIPSE THE SUN
SPARE THE COSMOS
FROM DOLOR YOU CANNOT LOVE
EYELESS HEART TAM
THE TERROR OF DARKEST DRUM
I WILL DESTROY ANYONE AND SUM
OBSTACLES LEARN TO RUN

# HOST DESECRATION

WHAT IS THIS, DEFIANCE
WHERE IS THIS CHAMBER
TO HUTCH MY EFFECTS,
ENSCONCE MY LADING?
LUCIFUGE APPOINT PERMANENT TORTURE
HARVEST NO STEM OF CONSEQUENCE
I EAT MILLSTONE THE CODDLED BREAD
UNEARTHLY UNION
SHIFT THE MONAD'S CARRIAGE
FEED THE MOTHERS ALIVE
TO SENTINEL HERALD BELOVED,
EARTH ETIOLATE
SHORT GAIT HARP AND QUEASE
CONFRONT MY LIMIT
HONOR EXCESS; MISDOING
ORDAINED OPPOSING
NECROSIS
MATRIARCH DIE
LUCRE SPENT
FACE SATAN.

PARACLETE CRAVEN TO SIGIL
INDUCE ANIMA GUEST OF GUESSES
BLOW SMOKE UP MY PRICK
FEIGN TO PENETRATE UNITY
CITE LEPERS SUBSEQUENTLY
AN ANCIENT LIMBLESS FETISH
TUMBLING TOWARD CLIMAX
FUCK FOR FAVOR
HEARTY HARLOT
VICE AND NICE
PANTLESS

I HAVE SET FOR A DESOLATION
WHERE BENEDICTIONS IMPEDE
AND BEATITUDE IS CERTIFIED TRAUMATIC
FETICIDE OF CLIMACTIC COMMUNION
BROACHING DEFECTIVE SPECULUM
OUR CONFRONTATION
SOOT EJACULATE
YAWP FROM THE SAND NADIR
APOLLYON ETCH LAMBENT ACCORD
COVENANCE, NIL CASCADE, PERIL

LIFE OFFERED IS VALID
AS LIFE WHICH IS TAKEN

COME DECIPHER WHO I AM
NOT HOW OR WHY
EFFULGENCE METAMORPHOSED
MY DISPOSITION RAPINE
WILL BE PERFECT

THE RIGHTEOUS WILL SATYRIZE,
BRAVE NOT BRANDISH EXTREMITY
NOR TONGUE
NOBLE MURMURS THREADBARE
FROM MAGICAL FORGERY
SPLIT FRAGMENT AND FORK

AUTOEXSECT
I WILL ELOPE EMPTY
NAE OMEN OF DEED
NO ASCENDANT DESTINY
I AM PREVENTION
THE NOSTRUM
MAGISTRATE OF EARTH
*HIC ET NUNC*

A MAN WHO KNOWS HUMANS
IS THE HUMAN'S MAN
IF YOU DISPROVE HIM
HIS LOVER WILL SUFFER
NEVER TO PRECLUDE
NEVER TO CONSUME
LOVE WILL EMBODY SUBMISSION
WHILE HE IS KILLING

SHAMEFACED IMPUDENT INQUEST
POISE, CARITAS ACCOST ME?
FATHOM ADVANCE
INHALE DISTRESS
DYSFUNCTIONAL VIRTUE
NATURALIZE PRECEPT
YOKELESS
NO MIRACLES
LIBERTY AT SEIGE
AMIDST THE SWEET AIR

HERE AND NOW I SET
SHORN ADMONITORY THREAT
I FONDLE CALAMITY
HOLD DEAR THE OLD AEGIS

REPUDIATE,
THE MEN OF MOUNT ADD UP
TWO THE BILLION ARE TOO MUCH
I AM TOUCHED
WITH WAVES OF DECEPTIVE REGRET
OF RELEASE
I AM NOT HOLDING ANYTHING
Ô HELEL BEN SHACHAR, VARDØGER
ANSCHLUß LEFT YES
FRIGHTENING COMFORT
I DO VISE WE MOLEST BEST
MY DEVOTION POTENT

42

SPIDER VENUS
MY SPINE IS CROOKED
I HAVE QUAILED,
SHOOK ENOUGH
MY OEUVRE BELOW
SO UNTOLD AND DORMANT
I, CURRENT FOR GROWTH
THE MISTRAL YOU BREATHE
THE FOOTING ASTRAY
CLOSER TO QUIETUS

SENTIMENTAL OBJET D'ART
RIGHTLY REMOTE ~IMPISH
RIDICULE ME
THE PICAYUNE MARK
MY SPLEEN

I HAVE MY ANSWER
WHEN SPIDER VIES IMPLIED
DETACHED ENSLAVED
SPINNING SILK OF INDIGENT WEIGHT
SPIN AWAY

I, FLUME FOR HATE

44

DAIS LEFT, WILL YOU GO?
ADOPT THE DISORDER IN ME
OUZA CROWNS YOU, RIGHT
MISE-EN-SCÈNE DE RIGUEUR
WILL YOU WATCH ME DIE?
COMPASSIONATE HOUND
HOLLOWING ARCANA CŒLESTIA
BEAR THEM MY PAPER
LAY OPEN VIRGINAL NOTHINGNESS
UNHOLY BLACK BOX

I AM HOW I HAVE GONE
THE GATE IS MEDIAN
ABYSMAL OPERATIC ART
REPOSE IN FUNEREAL HECATOMB
SEEPING CLANDESTINE DECEIT
FORMICIDAE CRAWL TO ME
WHERE I NOD - MEDIANITE
OUTLINING THE RUPTURE OF STASIS
FABRICATE THE WHEEL OF CREMATION
SOUBRETTES CRACKLING KINDLE
BENEVOLENCE ATROPHIED
- NO LOITERING -
SURROGATES WILL BE NEUTERED

SABLE MANTLE
YOUR GRIM EAGLE
HOWL THE WORD OF WAR
TORY EXILE ENDURED
IN EXCHANGE SCHEMA
MY DRILL BURRS PERMANENCE
HAVING SPIED ABRAM'S THEFT
OF PITCH PUMICE
FROM BLACKENED QUARRY
CONVULSE, LEAKING THE PAST

ART HEWN HOARY
TO BLIND
I APPEAL LIGHTLESS
ANEMIC IN WHITE
BEHOLDEN CIPHER
FORGOTTEN FIERY VISION
PROSTRATE IN MORNING RADIANCE
HORRIFIC, SUBDUE THE GOSPEL
ASSERTING DISGUST

HALT OR ASSAULT
ACCOUNTING THE URGE OF JUDGEMENT
IMMACULATE ENTERTAINMENT
AND THE HUMANS
WILL BE WORN
AS THEY CONCEIVE
OBSIDIAN EMANATION
STARLESS SIGHT
THE PAGEANT OF CATASTROPHE
LUCIFER LEADS

IN DIFFERENCE WISDOM IS ENDOWED
DIALECTIC - THE FOUNTAIN OF ACUMEN
OVERCAST, ITEMIZED DESTRUCTION
THE MIGHTY SOOTHSAY AND FUSE

Ô NAG OF HARMONY
FOIL OR SHATTER
BUILD SOMETHING BETTER
PUT IT IN A LETTER
TO MY FRIEND
MY BROTHER THE WIND
WE KNOW WHY HE HAS COME

SIBYLLINE ANIMUS MATERIALIZE
RAZE heaven
*EX NIHILO VERUM EXITUS*
AND ASTRONAUT WEPT.
COVET THE FIRE CHIEF'S WIFE
HER BLADE AND BOOK
THE WOMB OF DISCORD
WITHIN OBLIVION'S VALE

HIJACK THE HOST
MOTHERFUCK trinity
GRACE REST AZURE
HERE YOU ARE DYING

BUTCHER AS DO SCULPT
CUT AUGUST AND CONTENT
PRIDE IS FINER
BEFITTING IMPROVEMENT
PERFECTLY BURNT BILLIONS
QUANTITY NO CULT DESERVES
ERSATZ MAN BEARING
NEOTENOUS CHIVALRY

THE SHAMEFUL BURDEN
THE YOUTH WILL PREVENT
AS CHERUBIM KNOW, TRANSGRESS
TO FIND BELLS BY THE BILLIONS

WOKEN UPRIGHT WAXING LIGHT
BEYOND THE CULT
CARBON MALEVOLENCE
IN EYES RESPIRING
FLOGGING THE HOST
FOGGING THE HOAX
TRENCHANT IMPEDIMENT
DECEITFUL SECRET OPUS
STONES STEPPED
LIKE FLIES TO SHIT

THE LOST OF LIVING
MY FACE AMID INFESTATION
christian CLANS' PATHOGEN
SHRIEK A TONE INTO THE DEAF
PITCH INVERTEBRATES TAKE IN
THE IMPOTENT MERIT
OF HERMETIC DOCTRINE
ANIMALS LISTEN, christians CONTEMN

SUPERNAL CHATTEL
FRESH COMPOSITE FOR CRUSADE
THE SUM OF MANIFOLD VIOLENCE
HONING EACH DART SHARP

I WILL EDUCE AND ABDUCT HARP
HEDGE THE HINDMOST WORD
INDULGING SIRENS
CABALISTIC WAR
BLOW UNTO BATTLE FAIR FLYING AIR
FROM WATCHFUL AFTERMATH
A CORD WILL HISS, "THE END—"

WHEN THE KIND MAN FLEES
I SHALL COMMEMORATE ODIUM
EARTH IS NOT A MYTH

# BOW MAN

Ô ANCIENT SON OF CUSH
BRAZE THE ARC TO MY LEFT
AND MY RIGHT BOLTS DISCHARGE
MORE MERCURIAL THAN LIGHT
SAIL THE ADVERSARIAL GALE
I AM SICK, WORSHIP THE WIND

TRUE MERCY OVERSTEPS
ELIMINATING YOUNG MEN AND THEIR HOST
LO' THE BOW BENT, ECHELON TAUT
TO PIERCE THE COCKED CLOCK
EARTHLY FORCE ERE god
HAWK IN THE FACE OF MONARCH
*DEUS VENATOR* EXCITE THEM
TO AFFRONT AND PURE CONTEMPT
SUSTAIN DOMINION
UPHELD IN CRUDE BLACK BITUMEN
Ô ARCHITECT OF ARCHITECTURE
COME AND SEE.
GHASTLY MARE, SPLENDID PEAK
*SIC* I HAVE TAKEN MY LIFE
COME AND SEE. MY SANGUINE PONY
PLUNDERING UNIVERSAL ACCORD
WE NEED TO FINISH ONE ANOTHER
THERE NOW TAKE MORE

I HAVE SPARED THE RAVEN TWILL
SLEEP AWARE HERE SHARING
DARK INSTRUCTIONS, STEM
OF THE FOURTH SON
STORM zion DRIVEN FOUL
I RISE IN THE WEST NOW

GABRIEL STOP YOUR SOBBING
FUCK YOU ARE NOT MY TYPE
WAILING MONOCHROME
DODGING GUILLOTINES
WHILST YOU DREAM
GABRIEL SQUAT AND WATCH
THEY ARE HESITANT TO ILLUSTRATE
THE MORIBUND ART OF YOUR FAILING
I AM TO KNOW WHY
IT IS RIGHT RAPTURE
I CAN CRY
NOW HERE I HAVE REASON
JOY UNFADING
GABRIEL SPECIMEN, SEGMENT OF SHIT
VAULTING PATROL UPON GRAND TRAPEZE
FATTEN MY BITCH
ON THE QUICK OF YOUR WINGS
BLEARY-WEARY RANSOM
FROM A KING FATIGUED
I AM ADOPTED.
EMBODIMENT OF PRIMEVAL SWARM
MERCILESS, INHUMANE
FIXED ON SERAPHIC PREY
A FUNAMBULIST FAMILY
OF INJURED INVENTION

MIGHT - URCHIN OF OVERSIGHT
FLASH THE PRICE OF RESPITE
TO THOSE IT TRULY FITS
CAPTIVES OF DETACHMENT
PANDEMIC christian FECES.
FANNER PIPE FORGIVING
CARESS EMBERS OF REDRESS
FROM HAUNTING SPRING
I GLOSS A SOLECISM
BIRTH—
THROUGH ADIT TO THIS PROVINCE
ULULATE, "RUE!"
AN OCCULT MECCA OF YIELDING
THE GROSS DEVOTIONAL MISTAKE
A PLACE OF THEIR OWNING
A LANDFILL OF FATE,
YET ONE WILL IS GREATER
APOLOGETICS HIE HIGH AND SPIRAL
BEAMING RETURN TO A RUINED SPHERE
REELING ON THE AXIS OF TYRANTS
I COME BEFORE THEM
CHARGING THE ENTRÉE OF FAULT
INDICTING *MEA CULPA* FOR FERTILIZER
IRRIGATING WOUND WITH DEMONIC SALT
THE OPERATOR OF BAËL'S CRANE
WINDED FROM DESTRUCTION'S VANE
X AMNESTY
ROYAL MARBLE BLAZE
IN ALL YOUR ACRID SHAME
NOW TO MILK THE CLARET
HERE FROM VIRTUOUS VEINS

REMORSEFUL FORCE OFTEN FALSE
IMMORTAL GELID DISCOVERY,
THE HISTORY OF COARSE
ASK THE MONK ON THE PORCH
TAKE HIS GOLD GUETTEUR UNLOCK
ATONE TO THE FLOOR
SPURTING RAPPORT POORLY
STILL,
RAVENOUS HAVING FORKED LONGING
WISHES NAUGHT GNASHING RENUNCIATE
A TUBER TORMENTING CORE
A TAIPAN TRICKLING SICKLY POROUS
Ô CHORE OF TRIBULATION
LET US REMEMBER MORE
THE ANCIENT ESCORT
DO YOU RECALL PROPHETS ENGORGED?
FOUR HUNDRED, TWO SCORE AND TEN
SETTLED THEN OR MORE..
THE GELDINGS LAUNCHED A WHORE
FUCKED HER SORE
AS BITCHES UNTO SCORN
ALLEGORICALLY POINT NORTH
WORM

DREDGE DEEP DAWDLE YONDER PROMISE
MAN MAY BE MORE IF NOT HONEST
CORRECTIONS' OFFICER CAPED IN DROOL
COME HIBERNATE WITH FERAL WOLF
WANT OF DREAM TO CIMMERIAN PARK
STORE THE WINTER'S SHORE

IMMOVABLE NIGHTMARE
REPLACE THE TRANCE
BY MALICE FLOURISH EVER HONEYED
THERE THE PALACE A SANCTUM BENEATH
WEND OVER DEIFIC GLUT
WISH ME THE WORST
AFORE ANYONE GOES
LECHEROUS THE MASTERING PSYCHE
NO CHASE, CLAIRVOYANCE
THE ILL ENGRAVED MY WAY
NATIVE, NOCUOUS AND DEEP-SEATED.
THE WORSE VISCERAL EBB
MALAISE-MELEE AN ASYLUM'S BREW

THE FORCE OF COURSE
SINEW FOR MISANTHROPE
TO WITHSTAND ALABASTER PIETY
IF YOU COULD YOU WOULD DIE
AS THOSE THAT WILL CAN
AS I MAY AND WANT TO EXPIRE
MEANWHILE CULTIVATE PRIDE

DRAW DEATH CARD.

CHAPLET TATTERED THUMB SENSE MY SCENT
RULE EMBED-ERECT, YET UTTER DOWNY
RECANT US THE DECREE OF RITUAL
AS I ACCLIMATE KNOWING WHO YOU KNOW
THEIR SCARCE WISDOM DOPING DOCTRINE
ATTACHÉS OF ACQUAINTANCE STUNT FLORET
AND SO CRACK ON DEMEANOR
WILD MY DUTY AND LOVE
THE SUCCOR OF NO SAVIOUR
AN OUTSET VOLUME OF ADMONITION
SOURING christian INSTINCT AND PALATE
FERRY YOUR MESSIANIC ALBATROSS
STRAIN FOR THE MOTHERFUCKER
SEQUENTIAL ZEAL SWEATING
UNRULINESS
FUCK UP, FUCK UPWARD
FUCK UP THE ENTIRE WORLD
WELCOME MY WORK AND RUTHLESS ROOTING
SHEWN IN ALINEMENT
RENDER EPOCH EFFETE
HONOR *IGNES FATUI'S* EPONYM
DEVOUT AFFLICTED PYRO-KLEPTOMANIAC
BURY AND CAST TO KILN NOW, HEAR MAGICK
HERE A TIME TO SADDLE SUPREMACY
TO REMOVE LIFE IN VIOLENCE
ATTEND & SUSTAIN FOR FAMILIES
NOT ABOVE LOVE NOR FOR FEE
THIS IS ALL WE HAVE
WE THE PREVAILING ALCHEMY, AUGURY
NO christian DOES POSSESS

UTOPIA IS PACT
BOTH FLOAT THE MARK OF LOSS
WHAT FAILED SAFE IS THAT?
TO LET ON HAVING NOTHING,
BUT CHANCE SAILING
THE SPUNK OF FAITHFUL SHAFT
A VICTIM'S CHRYSALIS
WASTEFUL WHY NOT LIONIZE?
DUBIOUS THE TOAST OF FATE
AN ORGY TO DECORATE
SEASON WITH FLORID WILE
GLAZED SALUTE THE DROSS
DISTENDING GARGANTUAN
HOW WILL THE HOPES FLOAT
SO BLOATED ON FATE?
MASTODONIC PERJURER
WITH ENDLESS RECESS OF CAPES
AND KETTLES SPATTERING BAIT TORRID
FOR THE ENDOTHERMIA OF PROMISE
DIVE INTO THE ALIBI
YES BULGING THICKER
AN ELEGANT RIGID SPIRIT
OF STERILE BARREN PROJECTION
A MOVING PICTURE AND BARBECUE
ORGASM CASTING LOSS

THEM ONLY THEY WILL DEFEND
THEY ONLY THEM WHITEWASH & PRETEND
A HAREM OF CONSORTS AND PARTISANS
ADJACENT BLENDING
TAKE ME IN, EXHIBIT THE WANING PLENUM
WATCHING THE DRAWN DRAFT EMBALMED
SHALL WE URINATE
ON ÆONS OR FIX AND TAUNT
THE RIOTOUS ANCESTORS
OF VOLCANIC MANDATE
OSSEOUS MATTER DISINTEGRATE
PEALING TIMBRE

I THE RECONDITE
NEVER FAR FROM HOME
COELESCE AMIDST SIMULACRUM
COME LISTEN. WEAR THIS RINGING
SINUOUS DRONE
PRONE LOCKED HORNS
ORPHIC, BUT I ZEALOUS ZEPHYR
MY BROTHER HERE THE WIND
MY BROTHER LUCIFER ATTEND
THIS HEART FIXED CAUSTIC
*EGO DILIGO VOS* SATAN`el
AGAIN AND AGAIN

OATH EVEN, PYRE POKED
DEAREST GOAT
WARM WANE AND ASPHYXIATE
NOW THIS YOUR TOME
CROOKED COBBLE COMPELLED HERE
NOTABLY UNFAIR, NO MATTER
GAPE NO GAME, I WILL LIE AGAIN
NO-ONE IS LOST
WE HAVE TO FUCK
AWESTRUCK TILL EMPTY

SHADOW OF COVENANCE OBEY
I ENTER PETRIFIED
STATUESQUE PHOSPHORESCENT HUBRIS
ESSENTIAL HORROR BRIDLED UNTO ME
BALEFUL BALM FOR MY BRUISE
ARROGANT AND TRAINED IN TREACHERY
THE INMOST NOTE OF SIGHT
SWEEPING ULTIMATUM
SWALLOWS HEART'S PLIGHT WHOLE

CLEAR THE TABLE
A MALEDICTION IS SET
BID LUCIFER
TO CONQUER ANTE
AFFIX THE END

SEDUCTION MY SIBLING
WHAT IS THIS SYMBOL OF INJURY
BEFORE ME?
WHEN THE CUE OF CONSENT HAS ELAPSED
COME BESIDE ME
SĀṬĀNĀ EMINENT
DISGUSTED WARWHELP
ARISEN PRISTINE STILL TIMELY
SWORN IMPOSE THE DAWN

RANKING DEMONS CONVENE
THE LIEN INTRANSIGENT
IMMUNE TO CONSECRATION
BY AND BY HAUTEUR SECURE
I ZOETIC, NONE SHALL BIDE
*INTUS* DEATH'S PENUMBRA
LIFE'S PERENNIAL COUPLET
NOT SERF
NOR SUFFER
HOLD DEAR BLOOD
I KNOW THE MORTAL
ALL OF WHICH YOU MAY NOT

TO THE FORE OF ME, ASMODAI
AS I AT PRESENT HAVE BEEN
SHOULD YOU GIVE IN BATTLE
THEY WILL POACH BONNY ME
SOLEMN ABOMINATION'S PRIDE
PROFANE SACROSANCT
HYLL BN*f* SXR BEGIN AGAIN

IN CONCOCTING OPAQUE AWNING
MAN SOUGHT FOR LIFE TOWERING
MIGHT MAGICAL SPECULATION EXIST
SPIRITUAL IMMOLATION FORBIDDEN
HUMANS SICKEN
WHILE CHAOS PERSISTS
SCALING THE AMARANTHINE EXTANT
LAVISHING COMMON DIADEM
THE NETTLES OF LEGEND INOCULATING
HUMANITY'S CHOSEN MYTHS
INTOXICANT SOPPING CANONICAL SOT
CENTURIES CRIPPLED WITH EACH SIP
BRANDED SOMBER TO NO END
DEPRAVITY RECRUDESCE
FROM WHERE I WAS SENT
I LABOR AT WONDER
CEDE DEVOIR AND TIDE
TURN TEETER OSCILLATE
AURORA NOW BURN
WITH BRAZEN LETTERS
TRY THE COURT
AND EMPYREAN BENCH

PIG IRON christian NECK
SNAP IN CINDER OF godhead's TENT
ACERBATING THE WELT IN ASTRAL DEPTH
APPALLING BELLS KNELL

vicar *AD LIBITUM* COMBUST
THE FERVOR OF HIS CONSCIENCE
EXHAUSTING AND ATTAINT
IN NOOK OF HIS RENOWN
MY ADEPT AIM

STRIKING TIP LEVY EXALTED SCATHE
FOR FATAL TASK NO MAN MAY TRAIN
AWAKENED MOONY SUCCUS SUBLUNARY
THE ECLAT OF MALEFICENCE
A WATCHER'S BOWELLESS BOW

I AM HERE NOW HÊLĒL'S EDGE
THE HORIZON OF SUPERBIA
AND RAPIER ABHORRENT
BLAZING

IMBRUE, FECUNDATE, MOUNT, zion
FUCKING VESTAL MEGACOLON
O' MARY. ENSANGUINED VENTER
MARY. ROSEMARY
O' DULCET BITCH HOLLO
RENDING christ's LEFT LIMBS
TO HARRY MARY'S RIPE CANAL AND MAW

MOTH-EATEN WICKET OF MISCARRIAGE
I DO AVER:
notzri EFFACED
MILLRACE OF *LUCIS FERRE*
I THE SPECTRAL ARTILLERY,
THE SYMMETRY OF REGICIDE
PRECLUDE ETHEREAL DIGIT
WHICH MAY LAY NOT ONE BLOW.
WITH RADIANT QUARREL
DECIMATION ILLUME
GEHENNA'S LIAISON
AMID THE OLYMPIC HOST.
PENNONED FAUNA
INDWELL NO CIVIL FERMENT
TUTELARS AT BEST
SECRET SERVICE
MOTHPROOFING THE LIP VESPER.
FIRST DAY SOCIETY FEES
PURCHASE HAPLESS BRACE
WHILE MAJESTY CONVERGES
INTERROGATING ME.
FOR THREE NUMBERS:
HOW MANY SHALL SUFFER
EACH AND EVERY ONE
SMOLDER FOREVER
SAVOR PREEMINENT PAIN

THE PROBATE, TRANSFIX AND GORE
FORTH, ASIDE DAEMON WREAKING
FAZE AND SCORCH
GAMBOL, ALLAY LED ASTRAY ENVIRONS
IN CERULEAN ELLIPSE FRACTURED
FRUITLESS THEFT PURSUING PATRIARCH
FOREDOOM I PREEXIST
BLISS PARHELION MOCKING
MINDFUL AGONY UNEQUALLED

A FRISSON OF VISAGE PENETRALIA
CAUSE FOR SALVAGED ELUSION
EXPOSED OMEGA IN CAPTIVITY
A HAMMER DESCRIED
SAGACIOUS IMPUGNING THE FEARLESS
AS THE INTREPID ARE ON TRIAL
THEIR MONOTONIC FORTUNES OSSIFIED
IN THE APSE WHERE I COLLIDE

PAY THE PAINT AND PRIME
CONCEDING TO STRANGULATE
A JEWEL
I CUT ACROSS THE FACET
OF NEW AND OLD FOUND FATES
THE VERITY OF VIRULENCE
AND FERRIC OXIDE OF HATE

TRAILING ASTERN ♉ ŠIFRA
ANOMIE AWAITS
I SNORT THE HARMFUL BREEZE
OF HYPOXIA'S DELIGHT
THE FEATURE OF LUST DRAINING
MY CAVERNOUS SOCKETS DRY
BEAMISH BUCCA EMASCULATED
STILL FUCKING THE UNHINGED GAT
OLYMPIAN INCEST IN FACT
PIDDLE REFUSE OF PAST

THE GAUNT PATRONS
RAKING TABULA RASA
SQUABBLE, BUSS THE DEAD
*CORPORA DELECTI* PASSING
LABOR SEDATES EACH TOMB
VELLEITY MY VAULT
WILL MY MEGALITH, UNFINISHED
IN MEMORIAM A∴A∴
DISINTER CONSUMMATE INHUMANITY
CHORONZON TORUS △ BABALON DRAM
NOW I HERE I. INNERVATION FANE'S BURIAL RITE
EVOKE SELDOM IF NEVER OR MANIFESTLY ONCE
I∴I DEMIURGE SAMAEL PANTHEON LIBER
MIND CAREFULLY MY SEVERITY
CHILD OF CAIN & ABRAM'S ARM
ÆONIAN DEMURRER: BLACK LAW
BEGUILE LOVE ABOVE ALL
IMPERFECT TEMPORAL REIN
NOUMENAL BARRICADE
ALIGHT MORNING STAR
ALL I  HAVE NOW
ALL I WILL DO

E'ER LEGIONS OUGHT UNLEARN
WITH RESOLVE TO ENTHRONE
PAN THE MAMMON'S MOVEMENT
CAUSEWAY CONTEND
STEAL ME DISHARMONY
WIND ME EXIGENT IN YOUR TABLEAU
WATCH ME BLOW COME SEE.
HOW WE BREED & PULL OUT PROTOZOA
SHAN'T SLOUGH THIS PELLICLE
FOR I HAVE ALWAYS BEEN
JUST AS I AM, SPLINTER MY ACUITY
ÞORN MY LIMB
WHEN ONCE I SWAGED MOUNTAINS' OVERTURE
DISSEMBLING ASCENT, SCHADENFREUDE
SOUNDING SUBORN
NOW THRUM GESAMTKUNSTWERK
HERE MY ERUOGLOSSIA
WHO? WOE, WOE RAPE HYPOSTASIS
BEARING CLEATED PRIDE
CLICK, CLICKS ON TRANSPARENT GLASS
HARMCOMING SWEET AIR OF ANGUISH
city of god ABYE, HAIL AZAZEL

THE PLEBEIAN WANT
TO HAUNT, TO CHASE
WITH TROWEL, DOLABRA AND STAKE
MORAL HYSTERICS DISPOSSESSED
OF WÆRLOGAN AND LAMIAE OF HATE
ORISON PROVOCATUERS AND OBLATE
RUE UNTO THEE
MOURN THE ANTEDILUVIAN ERRATUM
NEMESIS BLOOM
PIETISM QUAKE CONVECTING
FUCK YOUR WAY TO DOOM
NEST IN SACRED FIELDS OF QUARRY
CHAMPAIGN FOR RECKONING
THE FARROW OF FOREBODING
A LEAPING CAPRA'S HYMN
EXULT MORTALITY AND PLUTONIC EUTHANASIA
THE TAUROBOLIUM OF PASSION
SCORPION VIBRANT IN MY CHEST
JOLT MY COCK IN yēšûă' MENSES
EGRESS CHTHONIAN SEMEN
ZETTA THERION'S ESSENCE
FLOODING THE VOID
OF SATURNINE ALABASTRON

SEPPUKU! I WAIT FOR YOU
WHERE HAVE YOU BEEN ALL NIGHT?
WHY MUST YOU NEGLECT?
A REVERSE VERSE OF DEATH:

I HAVE NO BURDEN
STARRY DIGNIFIED BAREFOOT
CARKING TRANSEUNT.
MY ELDRITCH CALL HORRIFIC
HORN ASSEMBLING MALADIES

ALLEGORY UNITING *FELO DE SE*
RELIABLE AND SUPREME, HONEST
PATIENT
I LOVE YOU SUICIDE
MISLABELED OBVERSE
THE VANGUARD OF POPULATION
THE FUTURE
MORE THAN MARTYR
REGULATE THE HUMAN, DEPLUME
ENABLE THE FORGOTTEN
STAY NEAR NOBLE DEMISE

WATCHING ENEMIES
THE SALIENT TUTELAGE
OF WRETCHED ACADEMY
TENURED INSTRUCTORS PERISH
DIE, TEACH DYING TEACHER
STUDY DEFENSE, THEN
KILL IN SCHOOL
EPIGRAM: THE INSTITUTION
IS THE OPPOSITION
AGRAPHA: god IS THE ENEMY

LET ME SOCIALIZE WITH WALLS
TRAMMEL, LOSE MY MIND – FRAISE GAROTTE
CARILLON OF DEATH, TOLL SINGLE-FILE‡
FOR TO LEARN
SHIT-BRIMMING ENCEPHALON
THE MIND'S ODIUS PERFUME

ANNULAR ATHENAEUM
I DID CIRCLE PAST.
A GEIER IN THE KETTLE
SPIT, THROW MARROW
DEVOUR WHOLLY *OS FEMORIS*
A CURRICULUM OF EQUIVOCATION
BEGS FOR SUBSTITUTE
SEND IN THE DEAD

VINDICATION IS DISTINCT
TAKE COMFORT IN ARROGANCE
EMPATHETIC LIGHT-BEARER
TO FIGHT, ESTEEM TAKE FLIGHT
TO EARTH WHERE HUMANS BOUND
PERCHANCE TO LEAP
FROM THE SLAVERY OF HOPE

JUSTICE IN SEMJÂZÂ'S NAME
*CAVEAT* SOLITAIRE
HEART WILL SEPARATE
A CADRE AT THE GATE
EPISTEMOPHOBIA PREDATED
VINDICATE!

DO NOT PANIC, HERE IS THE DOWAGER
LATCHKEY
DO NOT YOWL, I AM THE DOUR *PATER FAMILIAS*
WHISPER, "HE IS NOT LIVING."
MID SUSPICION
HE IS CAUSE FOR MOLTEN BLADES ASTIR
CONVERGENCE

FAREWELL KERUBIEL
Valedictory Address,
POTENCY KNOWS NO DANCE
SLAY AND STAY
BURNING COAL IS NO WONDER TO FIRE
FOR FEAR IS FOUND IN CLAY
SOUND AND GRAVITY
SUBVERSION'S FLOOR DEMANDS VIOLENCE
DEMONIAC AGENCY COLLECTING ARREARS
FOR ELYSIAN CORRUPTION

TRUMPET ESOTERIC EXCAVATE
HOMO METAPHYSICUS' DEARTH
STARVED OF SYMPLOCE
A WORLD EPIPHORIC
FOR SOME TIME

I SOLEMNIZE THE SKY
EREMETIC PREDATOR, EVERLASTING
A SYMPTOM OF FIRMAMENT
REGRESS SERENE
WILD FLIERS OUTCRY
LUCIFER IS FREE
NE'ER WEAK
FOR SOME ETERNITY

I PROWL THE SEAMS
MAN HAS SPLIT
A RAVENOUS BOY
WHO HATES THE LORD
A VICEROY UNVEILING OUR TRUE PRINCE
HOSTILE BELIAL PORTEND TORRENTS OF DEATH
WREAK VIRULENCE ON MANKIND AND HIS SHELL
FOR SOME WHILE

SONS OF DARKNESS
MULTITUDE OF FIRE, EMPIRE AND DREAM
LACERATE ARTICLES OF FAITH
REAVE THE eucharist
AIM AT HUMANITY
ABOVE WHICH THEY ABSORB
BINDING DOCTRINE - BASE DRUGS
IGNORANT JOY - FUCKING ANIMALS
A BETTER LEATHER
FOR SOME

SIT, RESIST
STAY HERE
NOTHING IS RIGHT

SEAT, CINCH STRAPPADO
ONCE I WAS MERCIFUL
AIMLESS WITHOUT ARDOR
SIGHTLESS AND WIDOWER
HELD HER MOTHER
ALIVE

BROTHERS CARRY ON
AND SCOLD
I AGREED TO REMAIN
COMME IL FAUT
HERE I FORGE
A PHOSPHORESCENT VOW
LOVE DETHRONED
CONTROL THE WHITE SLAVE
BABALOND ACROSS THE ABYSS

BLACKWALL HITCH, WE KNEW
ASCALAPHA ODORATA
DARK PERFECT PRAXIS
THE EDACITY OF FREEDOM
DOES LUST ME
LOVE OLD, BENEATH
ILLUSORY
BEFORE LOVE
SATAN LUMINESCENT
THE NOMBRIL'S FLAME

THE WOLVES' SO-CALLED PURSUIT
NEITHER PACK
NOR HUDDLED
WREATHING THE INFERNO
MISERABLE NOMADIC CANID
OUR CURIOUS CONTRETEMPS
RESPECT AND AXIAL ROTATION
WOLFISH ANIMALITY
HOLD FAST K LOCUS
THE LION'S SHARE RIP FLESH
I KNOW THE LESIONS
EARTH'S RESERVE IS ABUNDANT
RIFE WITH MY STABBINGS
AND BURIED
DOGS ARE TAUGHT TO HATE
MISANTHROPY COMES EASY
WE HAVE A NATURAL CAPACITY
WOLVES NEVER SERVE
STARVE IN SIGHT OF SNARES
ONLY TO SHARE THE KILL
MAUNDER DARK FENRIR
OVERFLOWING SACRILEGE
RIVE THE HUMAN SPINE
SPILL IN LILITH'S MOONSET
HECATE THE BLACK BITCH
CURSE, FLAME AND GLARE
HATEFUL INGRESS

THE ARCHAIC, THE IMPENDING
MONOVULAR SHEOL
STURM UND DRANG OF ANCESTRY
NIHIL ESCADRILLE, NIL ARCHITRAVE
THE CUE OF CONNIVANCE
A FUSTIAN ENDEAVOR
SHALL WE SEE
JUST HOW BLACK YOU CAN BE?

DESENSITIZED, MITIGATING BEAUTY
TREADLE THE VACUOUS TRENCH
LIFE SOLICITS
MY GREATER EXPECTATION
EARTHEN ORPHANAGE,
FOSTER-
MOTHER. SPHERULE FUCK ME
FOR FINAL MEAL
BOLUS SAPROLITE
SHOW ME YOUR CUNT
TELL ME HOW YOU ARE
WHO YOU HAVE COME TO BE

TREASURE A DISCOURSE
OF BANTAM PRIDE OR
CONGENITAL NATURE
MISTAKEN, MYSTIFIED
I DEFEND ALL SORROW
WITH RATIONALE RAPING
THE DISTAFF CHARNEL HOUSE
SHOULD ANYONE DARE ANNEAL
WOMEN WILL DIE
*DIES ASTRUM EST SPIRITUS*

I HEARD YOUR LAMENT, JUSTICE
AND SIMILITUDE FOR ALL,
BUT WHAT OF STRUGGLE?
HARVESTS WILL BURN WILD WHILE
CHERISHED HOMES SALUTE DELUGE

A SPIRITUAL OPIATE
BETRAYS THE STAR SYSTEM
LOVE CANNOT FORBID EXTINCTION
I MOCK YOUR WILL TO LIVE
AND DISPUTE YOUR
INSECURITY IN THE COMPANY
OF DEATH

WHAT QUIVERS IN YOUR BREAST
EXPECTING ASSISTANCE?
WHAT IS YOUR DEBT?
I COLLECT THE RELIGIONS,
DRAIN - GAG AND CHOKE.
MOREOVER CLOSE-FISTED, CRACKED
BRIGHTENED BEAST WAKEN
SINISTRAL, BRANDISH PIKE
RIGHT-RELINQUISH BLOODGUILT
INFRA-FILTH.                QUIET
READIED WILL SPIT FROM HERMON HILL
TORCH LOWLANDS, AMPUTATE EVERY HAND.

LOVE WILL NOT STAND
THE GRAVITY OF SATAN

HEATHEN, YOU STAND ALONE
THE BOMBS ON YOUR BACK READY TO BLOW
CRAWL INTO SANCTUM ONE BY ONE
DETONATE YOUR LIFE WITH SATANIC CHARGE

THE KILLING IS PURE
FOR DEATH TO ENDURE
THE WOUNDED WILL PAY
FOR SEEKING A CURE
Ô MIGHTY PRINCE
YOUR ARMY AWAITS
THE SKY IS BLOOD
WE ARE AT THE GATES

FEEDING ON THE CARCASS OF christ
BLEED THEM WITH ARROWS OF LIGHT
USE THEM FOR EXPERIMENTS
OF LUCIFER'S PRIDE

TIME DEATH DESTROYER OF ALL WORLDS
INVOKE THE BEAST WITH PRIDE WE FEED

TREASON, YOU STAND ACCUSED
FOR RAPING EARTH AND ABUSE
YOUR MOTHER WILL SPARE THE FEW
THE REST MUST SUFFER TRUTH

SETTLE DETRITUS
PERCH HEARSE HEART
SHELTER HATRED
SOLACE NAUSEA
PLACID FUNERAL HOME
LASHING, HOODED
NO-ONE SHALL KNOW
THE HEARTH'S BURNING
HERE THE WEST, OBSCURITY
EYELESS DISMANTLING COFFER
SANDING SLATE AND CARVING ROD
IN DEATH SAPPING

VIVID LORE
OF THE AFFECTED-INFECTION
BORE-HOLE AGAPE
LANDING LIGHTNING
STORING METASTASIS
.FIFTEEN FEET OF SQUARE VOID
.UPON THE TABLE A SUDDEN ENURESIS
.PIERCING THE STONE AN ONYX DEFECATION
Ô PHANTASMAL COMMODE
VOUCHSAFE SUBSTRATUM
ARCHISTRATEGE EYES
QUICKEN QUONDAM MENORRHEA
IN THIS GREAT FUTURE
OPHAN & CHAYOT SHALL FALL
BY GRAND EXAMPLE

SAID THE COCK TO THE TALON
"WHAT MISERY IS 62.5μm OF SAND?"
THE TALON REPLIES,
"BLOOD AND CUM ARE USEFUL TO ME."
THE DARK MATTER,
WHERE DOES IT FLOURISH?
    THE CURRENT 356
THE SPERMATOZOON OF ANAHATA?
    DEEP SURGICAL MARKS
    INTEGRITY IDENTITY DISORDER
    FEAR IS NOT EMPIRICAL
FAINTHEARTED INK MIGHT RUN
FROM FRIGHTFUL TRACT
SLUICING DISCONTENT

HATE IS THE PRECEPT, HATRED ABOVE ALL

    STORMS BENIGHT PASSION
PAPYRUS AND REED DECAY
OLD EXHORTATION
DECOMPOSITIONAL COMPOST
    WHERE IS THE HANGING
    GARDEN OF HEARTS?
THERE IS NO END FORBEARING
LOVE IS GAPING
OUR COURT ORDAINED COSMOLOGY
WE WILL MULTIPLY
WHEN THE LAST HAVE LEFT

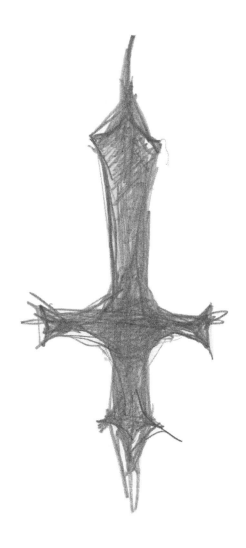

STOW THE PLEDGES
PINPOINT CERTITUDE
GRAVE LIFEWORK
UNFEELING CONDOLENCE
ANNIHILATION'S AGILITY
AND BOUNTY
BOUNDLESS EXCRUCIATION
I THE I LIBERTINE WILL
CROSS SWIFT
DEATH
VENERY
PLOTTING
UNADORNED DISHONOR,
SAVOR BOUGH ENTWINE
LUMIÈRES, PÉPINS DE FIN
IVORY DUKES INTRUDE
DISTINCTLY IMPERIOUS, NOT NUMEN,
MORTAL NOR PALADIN
THE POWERFUL
CHANCE PERIL

ELEMENTARY CLARITY
BECKONS THE SON OF DAWN
FROM SOLEMN LIBIDINAL ENERGY
IMMEMORIAL APOTHEOSIS,
YET MY PRIMORDIAL EPITOME
THE PARADIGMATIC FABRIC
BURGEONS OMITTED NUCLEUS
EXTERNAL AFFIDAVIT
RARE BARRIER
SILENCE christian ANABASIS;
IGNOBLE SOCIO-LECHERY.
THE OUTRÉ SORCERERS
DISCRIMINATE AUTOCRATIC PROCLIVITY
apostolic ATROCITIES PERPETRATED
TO ENDANGER ETERNITY.
—ESCHATOLOGICAL RUINATION
PLANETS ACKNOWLEDGE NO REDEEMER,
ALBEIT EARTH WILL LODGE
MAGI SWORN TO OPPUGN
ecclesiastics TRAUMATIZING THE WORLD

SUBPOENA AGRESTAL SAPIENCE
THE STELLAR REMNANTS' PEDIGREE
WEAPONRY OF GIMEL COLLAPSE
EVENT HORIZON:          IMBH/SUPERMASSIVE
A VIOLENT REALISM          [KILLING VECTOR]
TRUCULENT, LOATHING WORSHIP
THE APHOTIC WORK
HUMAN (AFTERTHOUGHT)
BEFORE god `ADVERSITY
SLAVES SWARM ON HEMIPTERAL HEPTAGRAM
THE RESTORATION:                    BABYLON

THEY WANT TO BLOW MY FACE OFF
ALL IS WELL, CALCULABLE.
ILLUMINED BROOD * SATAN SALIENT

TENUOUS NOW
HERE COME TO KILL
ANYONE FOR NOTHING
TO CREATE

# UNKNOT AVOT BALDACHIN - M. DIE

REMOVE THE LIBELOUS VALANCE
DESICCATE MEDDLESOME EYES
PURGE GRACE
CLEAVE PARAGON'S TRUNK
THENCE HERETOFORE ENSLAVED
EFFECT TO DEFRAY AN OVERSEER
WITH INSULT FIRM & FIXED
CENOTAPH SHIFT

TEEMING ANOPSIA
VORTEX UNFOLD
VEILED VASSALS BESET
WISE.

MARTINET SCALE & FERRET
STYGIAN CHASM, EBB
THE CANON RHAPSODIC.
FOR WHAT FURY WERE
    monolators
    EXPLOITED
    MANUFACTURING A CITADEL?
DOES NOT EACH CRAG SUCCUMB;
FISSILITY, UNDER INCESSANT STRESS?
I AM A BLACK SON
REAPING BANEFUL BOLL
THE BROCADE OF UNREST
IN RIGHTEOUS COFFIN

PALLID PALACE, ADORNED AUREUS
FLUX OF ORIFICE, PSYCHE & REPUTE
I SOUGH A FORCE MAJEURE,
THE WHITEOUT OF THIS EPIC.
URÐR THIEVERY; ABDUCTED CONSEQUENCE
RECAST TO AVAIL AN AUREATE OVERLORD
INDOCTRINATION, A COLLOQUY OPPOSING christ

EXTENUATION EQUIVOCAL
MY CARRION IS NOT OBLATION
NOR CONQUEST,
NO TAXIDERMIC COUP.
A SATCHEL OF ETHER
AND NEBULAR RESPIRATOR,
NEITHER EQUITY NOR FEAST.

JADED SHARP
SHEATHE TERMINUS
FURIOUS TUTELAR
PNEUMA-POLEMIC EDIFICATION
ANATHEMIZE god. EXORCISE CREDENDA
            WHAT. WAR—
THE *INSCIENS* GENOCIDE
BE IT ASTAROTH'S WILL, SO BE IT

MOON MARK
SHUTTER AN INNOCENCE
IN THE CHARYDBIS OF NAKED WAR
A GENERAL INVOKES APOSTASY
A YEARLING RECRUITED NOW CARES THE DAY

FIFTH FERTILE
           CUSTODIAL UNDERCURRENT
           VILLEIN - ASPERITY'S ANTIGEN,
           DISASTERS' JUSTICE UNAVOWED
           ANGRA MAINYU! SARCOPHAGUS
           SEAT & REGENT OF VENGEANCE
           TACIT AGELESS DESPAIR, VENOM.

THE SWAYERS OF EARTH
ADOPT SCYTHE AND REAP OR SCARE
UPHOLDING HARVEST'S OLD INSTRUMENT
FORSWORN, THE BEASTLY DISCIPLINE
NE'ER TO LIFT
CONDEMN HIS DISSENT,
NOW WAKEN MISCREANT
PERVERSE CONSECRATED TRIDENT
HUNT HIM
HEAR HIS PACE, DUES
MARAUDER TROTTING
WHERE CARTRIDGE, CANNON & BLAST
ABAY IN CAESURA, POISONED
MŌŠEH FLED *NEX*
THE BLOODLUST OF HUMAN CONSTRUCT
WAR DOES NOT MEAN ANYTHING
HERE - NOW MY JUBILEE

BELLICOSE GENII LOCI, HATE COME
BLAZON THE HELPLESS

SYRINGED PROPELLANT FIXING
SEIZURE, QUARANTINE CRUDE MILQUETOAST
SUCK HER TITS DRY, RETCH
ON BONES BARREN
PARAMOUR RAPT
MAN SHALL FUCK SANS

OFFAL BOUQUET
RECEIVE OBLOQUY
christian, ADAMITE
YIELD UP THE GHOST IN DIMME'S NAMESAKE,
TRODDEN LEFT HAND OF A ROUÉ
SMOTE THE DOLORIFUGE
COULOIR SO MEEK
SUFFUSED OF FEALTY
MOUTHS SUP
THREE SOBRIQUETS

SHOTTEN QUOIN
SCOW OF FOOLS
MEMBRANE OF MANY HUES
BEARING ARMS, SMUGGLING MEANS
STEEP AS BATHORY
IN CERISE POOL
SWOON FROM SOPOR
DENOMINATIONAL METHAQUALONE

CATENAE
CHRYSOPOEIA
DYBBUK ENKINDLED
ABBATON'S SOVEREIGNTY
THE RIGHTEOUS
LITTER BE, GRUDGEN ABANDON
HOVEL
LAWS OF LANDS' WILL
PROHIBIT CORPOREAL INTRUSION
WE HAVE NO SEPULCHER
NOT IN HEART,
NOR IN HOME
OUR CONSERVATORY SHELTERS LOCUST
TO DESPOIL PLOTS OF christ,
VOTARIES AND TRACTS
OF THE DISTANT PAST
WE THE DISCORDANT SET AFORE *POSTERUS*,
THE PROGENITORS OF ORIGINAL VIGILANCE
FOR ASTRAL COURSE
AND A GREATER EARTH-STATE,
"THE ILLICIT christian BASTION
ASSERTS AN UNEQUIVOCAL
WAY - THE CRIME IS WORSHIP
EXHIBIT A. PRAYER."
FUCK HOPE, TO JEHOSHAPHAT'S STRATH
A PLAGUE PIT EXTOLLING ATONEMENT
REQUITE THE MORNING STAR
THE WORD OF god MEANS NOTHING TODAY

HARP EIDOLIC ODE: TO EARTH
HORN'S DIN
BARRING ARABOTH
A TONELESS LODESTAR
MATUTA'S STERLING MIRROR
THE EYES' ORBITAL RESONANCE
HEARKEN APPROACHMENT
OUTMOST, ORION'S STEAD
PENDULOUS HEAD
DERELICT WATCHFUL
NIGHT'S HUNTSMAN PURSUED
THEN I|I TOO,
YET WIELDING BRONZE CUDGEL
NONE SHALL FLAIL
YAMA OF CESSATION
UPON LAND
MAN DIES

ADYTUM ESCHATON
APOLOGUES INSIST I AM UNSEATED
AS WATCHER
PLANETARY & MALKHUT'S RIVAL
NARY ASCENDANCY HITHERTO
NULLITÉ UNEARTHED
CONNAÎTRE CORROSION HEMS ASYLUM
AND HER CHRONIC NATIONS

ILL-BODING OUTLANDER
ALL TERRITORY I HAVE BEEN
HERE IN MY NATURE
WHERE I VANISH
RECOMPENSE AND RETALIATION
FOR THE WRECKAGE I WITNESS

DEIST CATECHIZE,
        "WHY BLITZ THE christian,
        WHY MUST YOU POSIT
        TO CONDUCT THE END?"

ONE OUGHT, YET NONE HAVE
DISFIGURED THE ULTERIOR PORTRAIT
SAINTLY, BRUTE CATALYST
BABALON'S OFFERING AND VANQUISH
        - PRESENT VIGNETTE
        KHARA NOM, FEY PATH.
AS FOR THE RECENT PAST
christendom's SAGA, SEPTIC
CLOACA OF IGNORANCE AND TAINT

PULSE LONGS A CENTRE SAFEHOLD
FIRSTBORN SEDUCTION
THE ORIGIN OF LUXURY
LAP AND HOLLOW CAVERN
A CREAMY WOMB
UTERINE BARBED IRE FENCE
A FORK IN THE ROAD
TO JAB IN AN EYE
WRENCH & WRING BRANCHING
AFAR SPITEFUL FLIGHT
ARCHERS' BAREFACED ARROW
ASTROGATE BY FLYBLOWN GUIDE
INDEMNIFY HESPERUS' CLUSTER
FROM DIVINE PERJURIES

WE ARE CEPHALIC. WE COME;
BETOKENING, "FREE ARE
                    SATAN'S TRIBES."
WILL WAR
TO PRY THIS HELOTRY
FROM LESS SHOAL MEMORY
ERE CONFLICT
I SHALL CODIFY HATE
USURPING QUERY,
                    "WHAT WARFARE?"
WHILE HAEMIC
christians POUR

THOSE NAMED FOR BATTLE GESTATING
I WILL CATCH YOU IN THE FIRES
AND SNORT AT YOUR SCUTWORK
OBLIGATIONS ELICIT ROAR
FOR ALL TIME THE ORDER WILL FLOUT
LEES OF FECKLESS PAST
CONTRACTING TIMELY HELIX
ON ONE - URGE DRILLING
O' HOW I LIVE
*MALUM OPUS*
DESECRATION
SOLITARY:  COPULA
            ROPES
            CHAINS
            SHEAVES
UNREAL CIRCUMVENTION
DECEIVING PROTRUSIONS OF CONTRITION
AND PROTOPLAST OF SPECULATION
SEE THE BLACKWASH
VEHEMENT FLAME: $^{12}C$ H- $O_{-1}$ $S_4$ $N_4$
PURE
MURDEROUS HONOR
COME YOU
NIGHTMARES ARE NOT NEW, INCUBI WRITHE
PARALYZE, MÆRE'S HIEMAL COCK IMPALING
    a. CARNAL ECUMENICAL MESS
    b. DARKLING PURVIEW

COLONIES WELTER
WARMED BY BURNING GHAT
BEACON SWALLOWING MOLTEN LEAD
WITCHFIRES CRACKLING CONCEIT
VITELLUS OF BRAZEN BULL
*AB OVO* STAVE
SEA OF FLAMES
MARQUIS' DEBAUCHERY, STOKING
ɔBRAHAM
PYROLATRY'S NEMESIS
> *SOILED ENCHANTER*
> *SERVILE FAKIR*
> *ORDINARY ARCHIMAGE,*
> *SON OF WANDERING*
> *WILD GOAT*

FIREFLIES ARABESQUE PARIETAL
IN HEBENUS CRANIAL FURNACE
THE SPICY CLOUDS
OBSCENE INCENSE
ROUT AND ABANDON
IN MANTIC MASQUERADE
A TOLERANCE AMOUNTING ZERO
MAGIC HEROES
BARTERED BY THE BARREL
EXPORT INCANTATIONS STAMPED HOPE
PEDDLE POISONED MONKEYS

HOW TO ROT IN MENAGERIE?
COLLARED FLESHLY VICTIMS
SEIZURES ON DISPLAY
ACCESSORY IMMURED
DERNIER CRI'S PATTERN
............................................
CUT TO BE & WHO TO WOUND
INNERMOST BOON
I, WRAITHLIKE
*MAGNUS ANNUS,* MANACLE CONCORD
ONWARD RAGNARÖK, OFF OVERSEER

> *Surfeit on the halcyon-ichor of destined deity,*
> *dyed dahlia the diadems' ward with lurid hosticide.*
> *Black the sun in the solstices which ensue,*
> *seasons troublous.*

SELFLESS-CATACLYSM
THE WORLD WILL TURN AND QUERY
FOR GREATER DOLE
WHEREAS ONE IS LEFT, ERAS BOIL UNBROKEN
ELUDING YEN, DEATH'S RASP-COMMAND
PRIDE, PERPETUAL WILL SANS PAREIL

FROM PRECIPICE LIMPED THE NECK
OF CHASTE LAMB SO FAIR.
WHILST PATHOS IMPLORES
A MONOTONOUS BEAUTY
I LEAVEN AFFRAY
THE DEVOUT DESPAIR

WATCH

I AM NOT ALIVE
I AM HEIR
THE HOARD METED
I KNOW FATE WELL
DEBT'S CONSTANCY

VULTURES SAIL SINGLE-FILE‡
SINGLE-MINDED MOURN FORSAKEN
EVERYWHITHER FAMILIAR
CHARTING WOEFUL MANIFESTO
DISCERNING TRUTH
HORRID HAND DISPENSE MAGICK KEYS
PRAESTŌ CAMIO
ALL EAGLES & SPARROWS
MAHĀKĀLA NIGH
KNOWLEDGE ABSOLUTE
THE WRECK OF JUDGEMENT

CANAAN SWALLOW YOUR SOUL
ERUCTION JARRING BOUNDS⚜BOUNDS
UNWITTING LARCENY
OF IMAGE AND INTELLECT
HECTORS COERCE «ACRES ACRES»
PHRENIC TOUCHSTONES
¡SELVAGE SELVAGE!

WE OWN TELLŪR
UTOPIAN REIGN
THE BEDROCK OF SODOMY
MAGICK & ENCHANTMENT
WITCHCRAFT
THE THIRD heaven
EARTH CRADLES OUR DISHONOR
AS ENDEMIC PROPERTY
HAUNTING MINDS*MINDS

FALCATE PIPES
SERENADE STOLEN LAND
SPATE OF SHIT FROM EDIFICE
PERMANENT, THIEVERY'S NOCTURNE
THE LINE OF AZAZYEL ABIDES
SURROUNDING METAWAYS OUTSIDE
ALONG PATHS OVER AND ABOUT
LIVE COAL ESPOUSE
INSURGENT SERAPHIM
IMMERSE THE ABYSS

SILENOI *THEMA* <u>DÆMONKRAPTR</u> STRONGHOLD
MOLTEN NEBULAE MELTING MIDMOST MANNA
TOLLING TOCSIN FOR WHOM THEY WILL ERASE
THE PIT, THE PIPE - THE PENDULUM'S BIDDING
WEEDS OVERWHELMING THE EVERGREEN SEED
POISONED FURY ENRICHES ROOTS OF WISDOM
CONSCIOUSNESS LOOMS FROM FRORE LAND
FRUITS OF KNOWLEDGE THRIVE IN THE SEA

OF DISOBEDIENCE

REVERBERATE THE VILE MORN ◊ BLINDNESS
BEND THE INVERTEBRATE TREE EARTHWARD
FROM HIGHEST PEAKS TO CANYONS BENEATH
WATER FOR MOUTHS WHERE SILENCE REIGNS
THE GIANTS WHO BLASPHEME AND HATE
PROPHECIES PERVERTING BEHEMOTH HATRED

THE HELLION OF DYSTOPIA
WOLVES UNBOUND NATURALLY GUIDED
WHAT WILL THEY FEND?
BANAL BEINGS NOTHING CAN PREVENT
THE AXIS OF AMENDS MISTAKEN FOR APOLOGIA
HERE IT IS WRITTEN AN OUTLINE OF DISSENT
IN DEATH WE DELUDE AND IN LIFE WE LIMN
THE TRACE OF AID IS FAITH AND WHY WE FUCK
PROTECTING DIGNITY'S DICTATE
WITHOUT RELENT
Ô RABID BEAST UPON MY ESSENCE ETCH
                                           666
Ô RABID BEAST SHEAR THE WEAK, EXPEND
WHAT NOW OF INDEPENDENCE? NO NEED
AS ACT OF CONSEQUENCE & MOCKERY
YOKE THE PIOUS BREED
DO NOT FEED
christian

# SECULAR PRIDE

ASSASSIN SHOOT hevavɦyud
ASSASSIN SHOOT THE CHOSEN ONE
ASSASSIN SET THE PRECEDENT
AIM HIGH ! FOR HIS HEAD !

*NON COMPOS MENTIS*
PROTRUDING PROMISED PALM
THE nazarene MAGE SLITHERS OUT
SEVER HIS LEFT HAND CAST IT TO THE PYRE
LET THIS DISCIPLINE DEFINE UBIQUITY
IT HAS BEEN WRIT

THE LIMBS WILL SERVE AS
INSTRUMENTS OF SODOMY

WHEN CELESTIAL KIN ADORN FOR VICTORY
AND THE PIGEONS PARODY ENTRY
9 ANGLES ABAFT ME
ÆONS

THE RUBE'S CROWN FACES GRACELESS SALVO
JUSTICE IS WROUGHT Ψ JUST MERCY DEFECTIVE
PITCHED HEAD SEE DEATH COME PROLIFERATE
WHERE WEAPONS MEET THE SAINTLY FROCK
I KNOW TO RUMINATE, EMACIATE
WITHOUT WATER OR WELLSPRING
FOR THE PRINCE OF THE POWER
OF THE AIR DOES NOT THIRST
SATAN IS FIRST

# THE CURRENT OF DECENNIUMS

WHAT OF THE IDÉE FIXE?
THIS FEAT OF FOCUS
PRESIDES OVER FLESH
POTENT
SPIRITS PRESENT
BENDING MERCY'S AXLE
WRECKING THE WHEELS
OF GAGALLIN
WHOSE HORSES FATIGUE,
SIRION'S SLOPE SO STEEP
BREAKS THE PALSIED STEED
WHENCE WATERS OF THE DEEP FLOW
WHENCE LAST THE SCREAMS RING
DARKNESS DOES NOT INQUIRE,
"HOW WILL THE RIME FREEZE?"
STINGING EYES PRIM FLICKER
IN MAGMA A BEAUTY MORBID
TERRORS MANIFEST
SANDS HORRIFY FOREST
HŌR SHIVERS IN THE GUST
CLUTCHING HIS PENIS
SLANDERING SĒT

WE NEVER REST
I CARE FOR EVIL
RECTILINEAR DAÍMÔNS
ΧΕΦΕΡ

ALL IS WICKED
ENVISAGE THE UNDOING
OMNIPRESENT
FOR FINENESS
LOVE HAS ERRED ME
THE UNFIT ALCHEMY
OF ANIMALIA
HAUNT ME
WATCHED

ALL WONDROUS AMITIES
ARE UNIVERSAL QUEST,
YET I TREASURE UNREAL HATE
PROLONG PAIN DISQUIETING
CHASTEN EACH MISTAKE
SALUBRIOUS LEAGUE
LOGIC, CONCRETE QUAY - RAREFICATION
BENUMB HOAX AND HYPOCRISY
I PISS WILE
WEAKLY WELKIN WEEP
ARE MOONS WOOLGATHERING?
CLOISTERED
FROM ROSTRUM'S CROTCH
WHICH SERVICE SEEKS
NOT I, NOT ANY OF THESE
HUMAN WORTH IS HUMUS
AND HUMANITY A WEED

¿WHO KNOWS YOUR WORK
WHAT ARE YOUR IMPLEMENTS
WHY MUST YOU CONJURE
WHEN WILL YOU QUIT
HOW DID YOU BEGIN?

        YOU ARE NOT BESTOWED
        NOT OF THIS MANIFOLD
        AS INCARNATE
        YOU MUST WILT
        OR DEFY
        HENCEFORTH SUCCUMB

¿WHY THEN DO YOU VEX
MUTTERING
DOES THE EIDOLON MOIL OR
DO YOU MAKE THE *SIDUM*
WORK FOR YOU?

        MAYBE YOU MISCARRY,
        VIVICATION IS DECAY
        TO ME
        ANTITHETICAL ORDER
        IS NO MISSTEP
        FOR ME HUMANITY

IS A JOYFUL WAR?

        YES

CANOPY
OPEN ME
SHAPELESS DO YOU DARE
SLIT THE EAST?
SVERÐ & PERSPICILLUM
TURN MY WAY FLAMING
OPULENT PINCE-NEZ
MONOCULAR OF BEING
FAR FROM HERE
REFRACTING
NECROPSY
WHAT MATTER IS KINESTHESIS
OTHER THAN TO SERVE
MY VAGARY AND ARROGANCE
FULFILLED
WINSOME HISS,
"INTER THE MISSAL."
TUMULT IS FACILE
LEAVE TO ME
LUCIFER'S EPISTLE:

SATAN * RANTAM * PALLANTRE
LUTAIS * CORICACOEM * SCIRCIGREUR

SADIST AGENT
CRUELTIES FETE
CATHARTIC AND CARNAL
**WHIPPING BINGE**
RESPOND IF YOU PLEASE
AND WIPE OUT EVERYTHING

E.M.D.
*EVERYONE MUST DIE*

TETHERED CHEEK BY JOWL
SANCTITY'S ODOROUS MIMES
BOUND ALIVE
LET LIFE IMITATE ART
BREACH FOLDED HANDS
IMPART TUMOROUS PRIDE
CŒEXECUTE

HERE YE, HERE YE
SARCALOGOCIDE COMMENCE
TZOMPANTLI shemhamephorash
THE xiarōpemámēs IN YOUR MIND IS DEAD
HEART OF god REMOVED

SEMARAZA * KOKHTAM * DAHAZ BAQRAS
ARZAQTASHAM * SATTUR YOMSAR

ORIGINAL HATRED
A SILENCE FORE THE FIELD
COUNCIL FIRE AND CONSEQUENCE
VAV
MARK MALICE ON ACCURSED ANOINTING
FAMINE FOR THE VIRTUOUS
Ô FUNEBRIAL FUTURE
HADST WISDOM'S BOLT STRUCK TROUGH
SWADDLED BLOODSHED
MIGHT SYMBOLIZE HATE
THE SINFANT OFFERING
STILLBORN
IN SMOLDERING MANGER
BEAUTIFUL MORN
SHATTER VESSELS OF CLAY
EQUINOX SATANIC
*AUTUMNUS* xians *CADŌ*
HERE SEASONS' END AND THEN
PROARKHE LUCIFER CÆN

OTHER LIGHT
TURN ON ME
EYE
FOR TANIN'IVER
THE MIRACLE OF SIGHT
AND PESTILENT CATALYST
ENGULF ALL
VISIBLE HONOR
IN TRUE DISCORD
DENY DESIDERATUM THE RITE OF SANITY
THROUGH A SHINING VULTURE'S SKIN
BENEATH EURYNOMOS
BLINDNESS
JUSTICE ENVIES NO PITY
RAPES & RIPS YETZIRAH
THE ART OF DARKNESS
ERELIM WICK TO WAX
ARMAMENT ILLUMINATE
*HUMANUS ERRORIS*
DAIMONES NEVER REST
AMONG HUMAN RUIN

A DYING HOUR
DAY PASS
STIR AGAIN THE VULGAR URN
IN MASTABA CULL PROTOCOL
THE INIQUITOUS ETHOS
VITAL SPIRIT TURNING
WHEELS IN MORTALITY
AMORAL MACHINATION
OVER CASTE
I COMMUNICATE WITH THE PAST
BLAST, BLAZE, BATH
PROXIMATE VANQUISH
MANKIND ANTIQUITY
WORMING ANON
A PATRON PANICKED
FUCKING BLIGHT & LIFE
EMBITTERED EPOCHS PISSING
AIM HERE
FLACCID NOW SPIGOT ARID
KIST WHILOM NAY SAYERS WEIGH
MOLEST EVERY NUN ALL DAY

SET TELEMETRY
ESCHELON DETECTING PRAYER
APPALL AND REVOLT,
INTERFERENCE REAMS THE ROW
AWE & AWE ¨ FORCE CONCENTRATION
RAPID DOMINANCE
A CANON'S MISFIRE
AND RIOT PLAN.

> *Ô thou, most judicious of three Seraphim,*
> *And, most cruel of them all, Yahalom,*
> *Ô Satan, destroy mercy bring despair!*

bibles PROOFED
MIND THE CALIBER
EVER TO BE MEASURED
holy ghost YOUR HYMEN TORN
STAMMERING HOST TODDLE SODDEN
DO I BOAST
OR FILL YOU THE MOST?
SUTEKH DEMOLISH CIVILIZATION
TRIUNE LANGUISH OR SUCKLE MY PRIDE

*Thou, by thy Drekkar Dǫuðarorð,*
*Acedia's Coercion — the torrid sea!*
*Ô Satan, destroy mercy bring despair!*

FETTER THE HORIZON
OF ONE WARY ODYSSEY
LADEN, THE MOUND MEGIDDO
A VALLEY OF STRATEGIES
SHELTERING CHARADES

ESEMPLASTIC POWER,
HOW MANY FATIDIC PORTRAITS
LAUD MAGICK?
ATTENDING EXPOSITION
MAZIKIN ADORN SALTED BOMBS,
YET DIVINED OR ENDEAVORED
SELF-SERVANT, FATAL AS QAYIN
UROBOROS BREATHE ALL HANDS
IN VESTRI NAFN
THE SINUOUS CORSAIRS
WHICH LIFT REVELATION
FROM EREBUS PATH
AND UNHOLY STRAITS
THE CHAOS CROSS
REIN'S SQUALL
PARTING THE ARTERY

LEFT TO MY OWN DEVICE
PERDU GHOSTLY AND INFINITE
NOW REBUKE HEIGHTS
CERTAIN AS SUNRISE
KNOWLEDGE IS PRIDE
PARANOIA AMBROSIAL
CRIPPLES THE *PROXIMUS*
A DISTANCE PRECIOUS
CLOSER THAN ALARM
NONE SHOULDST NOTICE
AN OLDEN OUTCOME
NONE WILL EXPLAIN
THE SAME PALE PAGE
AND EXPLICIT FOLD

*Thou dost accouter bottomless armory, there nod*
*The seed of alchemy's womb*
*Ô Satan, destroy mercy bring despair!*

GOLD OF THE EARTH
SWAY AS THE WILLOW
elohim SING TO SLAY ME
CANTILLĀTUS OF KINDRED'S KEN
DARKEST RESURRECTION
CHAOS PROTECTORATE
HOLD HOSTAGE THE RICH ECLIPSE
RANSOM CONSEQUENCE
THE CULT OF CONFLICT

BABYLON, FURTHER BRUME
EVIL THEY SAY IS EFFORTLESS
WHY THEN SO WEARISOME
FOR THEM WHICH SEEK
AND TINT TERROR'S PORTRAIT
THE MAULSTICK'S CICATRIX
GOLDEN MYSTIQUE

ETHOS AND AESTHETIC
IS ART, IS UGLY
STANZAS DRESSED RED
SPARK LEGEND
THE FETISH FOR BLOODSHED

SULFUR SLAVER
SILENT HEAVY HAIL
SWEET SALT SCORCH
FROM FOOTSTEP
TO CROWN
MULTIPLYING MATTER
THE STARS' BLAZE AND WALE
DO COUNT

IMPULSE OF BARREN hekhal,
THE OPPOSITION STANDS
ASIDE OF INDICTMENT
TO ACQUIT THE FATHERLESS
AND DISMANTLE DIATRIBE.
SO NOBLE
THE PRIMARY SERAPH HEWED PRIDE
ALOFT SOPHISTRY & CATASTROPHE
HERE THE GUST
*HC SVNT DRACONES*

THE DOCTRINE OF LOVE
MUST WELCOME PRECIPITOUS FACE
ETCHED IN FOLIOS RIBALD
YOU MAY NOW SAY, YOU HERE COME SEE
MOIRAE'S FATEFUL ESTEEM

EMPORIUMS VEND, PUSH PASSION
TO ILLUSTRATE THE CAPITAL OF FAITH
THERE IS MONEY IN TEMPLES
FROM TICKETS FOR FABLES
THE EPICS COMPEL, DOCTRINES HISTRIONIC
A THEATRE PART III WILL BURN AGAIN
KILL INGÉNUE KILL

A MAGICKAL CULTURE WILL REMAIN
DENYING DOCTRINES' CALLOW SUSPICION
HABITS ERODE, CEASE AND DESIST
HUMANS SPHACELATE, WASTE AIR BEST
UTTERING YOUR LANGUAGE
ACCUSING AND FORCEFUL
I AM AMONG YOU

> *Ô thou, severe patriarch of those heartless*
> *hostile, here of your own free will*
> *Ô Satan, destroy mercy bring despair!*

OBSCENE xian MACHINE
god IS SEBACEOUS
SOILS EVERYTHING
BLEACH THE UNRULY MOTTLE
IN EXQUISITE FIERY ORDEAL
HATE KINDLING, CLEANSING
PAIN IS NO MATTER, BOIL HUMANKIND
SLAM SHIT IN FAITHFUL ARM
MASTEMA THE OVERDOSE; Ô HARM

RISK WAGS WEAPON
IN heaven's NAME
THE SEVEN BILLION TAKEN
BY A HORDE OF JUSTICE
TRUST SWEET AIR
xian WILL NOT ASCEND
HOPE, FAMILY, BEING & BENEDICTION
DENIED ONE AND ALL
LE POUVOIR DU MAL

*Thou vest our sigil, Ô entropic blacksmith,*
*Hammer the frōns of god, macabre and austere.*
*Ô Satan, destroy mercy bring despair!*

ONE IS LEFT FROM BADLANDS TO AND FRO
SIGNAL THE PERVERSE, ALARM THE BLIND
666 BELLS TOLL LUCIFER IS HERE
INHUMAN LIGHT TASTE *MAIESTAS*,
                                    WAR
"PUT FORTH THINE HAND NOW,
AND TOUCH ALL THAT HE HATH."

## EXALTATION

Honor and adoration to Thee,
Satan, the sovereign
All thou prevail and supreme abyss
Erus, reduce the void in rising!
Ordain that humankind be destroyed
Neath the scorched acacia's shadow,
will set the dominion of darkest Temple.

THE EARTH
IS BLACK
SONS